Remembering
Louisiana

Dean M. Shapiro

TURNER

PUBLISHING COMPANY

Front Street in Alexandria is seen in this 1891 image. The iron lace–styled balconies on two of the buildings resemble those of the New Orleans French Quarter and attest to the city's diverse cultural heritage. Located in the center of the state on the Red River, Alexandria is the hub of the state's "Cross Currents" section—a transitional region between the predominantly French Cajun southern parishes and the more typically Anglo-Saxon parishes of northern Louisiana.

Remembering
Louisiana

Turner Publishing Company
4507 Charlotte Avenue • Suite 100
Nashville, Tennessee 37209
(615) 255-2665

Remembering Louisiana

www.turnerpublishing.com

Library of Congress Control Number: 2011929756

ISBN: 978-1-59652-837-6

Printed in the United States of America

ISBN: 978-1-68336-852-6 (pbk)

CONTENTS

In this 1893 photograph taken in the town of Opelousas, a group of men stand around the front of the J. B. Sandoz store, which specialized in horse-drawn carriages and accessories. The parish seat of St. Landry Parish, Opelousas was founded in 1720 and is the third-oldest city in the state, after Natchitoches and New Orleans. Today it is the home of three large festivals, the Original Southwest Louisiana Zydeco Festival, the Yambilee Festival, and the Opelousas Spice and Music Festival.

Acknowledgments

This volume, *Remembering Louisiana,* would not have been possible without the diligent efforts, over many years, of the dedicated staff and volunteers at the Onondaga Historical Association. Past OHA director Richard N. Wright's work with the photography collection should be especially noted, and the current assistance of archivist Michael Flanagan is greatly appreciated.

PREFACE

For the past 300 years—from its earliest remote settlements to the present time—Louisiana has been one of the most fascinating and culturally diverse locales on the North American continent. And one of the least-known-about, until relatively recent years. With sizable sections of the state largely inaccessible until well into the twentieth century, much of Louisiana grew up with a degree of isolation that allowed it to nurture an indigenous culture unlike anywhere else in the United States.

However, the state's strategic location at the southern end of the most important waterway on the continent virtually guaranteed that it would grow and develop into a crossroads of cultures and a center of commerce. From the roots of the tiny, precariously situated outpost near the mouth of the Mississippi River named La Nouvelle Orléans by its French founders, a great city would emerge and become a bone of contention between three European powers and a newly developing American nation. And with the waves of various nationalities that swept in from Europe, Africa, the West Indies, and elsewhere in the New World, a veritable gumbo of cultures would give New Orleans and Louisiana a unique, multidimensional flavor.

Natchitoches, founded in 1714, gave France a foothold in the northwestern quadrant of its recently claimed territory, while New Orleans, founded four years later, gave the French an anchor in the southern region from which to move goods and people to and from the mother country. French-speaking Acadian exiles (nicknamed Cajuns) from the British-conquered eastern provinces of Canada found their way to the remote bayous of southern Louisiana in the mid-to late eighteenth century. They settled into lives of fishing, trapping, and light farming where conditions permitted. Other nationalities followed closely behind them. Among them were the Spanish who took control of the territory in the 1760s, Germans who tilled the rich alluvial soil along the lower reaches of the river, and free people of color who made their way from the Caribbean into the port of New Orleans and pursued vocations available to them at the time. Intermarriage between these groups and those of French descent resulted in a distinct Creole class that, for many years, dominated a large segment of New Orleans society.

By the time Louisiana passed into American hands, thanks to the Louisiana Purchase (which was signed in New Orleans in 1803), the stage was already set for the varied crosscurrents of culture to begin interacting and creating a new dynamic that stood out in contrast with the rest of a largely homogeneous nation. A multiplicity of languages, customs, cuisines, forms of entertainment, and artistic and architectural styles merged into a whole whose parts were distinct from one another yet inextricably interrelated.

Religion played a leading role in the growth, development, and melding of Louisiana, both before statehood in 1812 and afterward. Catholic church jurisdictional divisions known as "parishes" came to define the boundaries of geographical entities termed "counties" nearly everywhere else in the United States. Churches were the focal points of whole communities, spiritually as well as socially. Large-scale festivals like Mardi Gras in New Orleans and its surrounding areas have their roots in religious traditions. In the predominantly Baptist parishes of northern Louisiana, the Baptist church imbued the region with a strong work ethic that helped it to grow and prosper as well.

The twentieth century brought great changes to Louisiana, although more slowly to some regions of the state than others. The discovery of oil in northwestern Louisiana accelerated the pace of modernization there. No sooner did those reserves begin to run dry than large undersea oil deposits were discovered and tapped in the Gulf of Mexico, helping the state's southern region to enjoy its own measure of prosperity. Concurrent with the oil boom in the Gulf, the isolation of the bayou country finally came to an end. Roads and power lines brought modern conveniences to those who, for centuries, had been self-sufficient and insular. New Orleans developed into a great import-export hub for international trade. With tourism, music of all genres, and haute cuisine adding to the mix, Louisiana began playing host to millions of curious visitors of all nationalities.

In the pages that follow, the growth and development of Louisiana can be seen pictorially from the 1860s to the 1960s. Louisiana was more resistant than most other states to giving up its old ways, its customs, and its priceless architectural inventory. And as time has proven in many cases, it didn't have to. Many of the old buildings seen in this book still stand. Many of the old customs still prevail. Many of the old traditions are still observed. The new coexists with the old. These are among the unique characteristics that make Louisiana such an intriguing place to this day.

—*Dean M. Shapiro*

A statue of statesman Henry Clay stands in the middle of New Orleans' Canal Street in this photograph from around 1865. It was created by Joel T. Hart and dedicated in 1860. Clay, "the Great Compromiser," was revered in the South for his efforts to strike a balance in Congress between the slaveholding and free states. A street in uptown New Orleans is named for him. The statue was alter move to Lafayette Square.

RECONSTRUCTION AND RETURN TO NORMALITY

(1865–1899)

This 1867 image shows the lighthouse at Southwest Pass, the farthest south of several mouths of the Mississippi River. Also seen are the lighthouse keeper's house and the wooden boardwalk leading up to it. The second such brick structure to be built in that location, it was ill-adapted for its swampy base and soon began leaning dangerously like its predecessor. It was replaced in 1871 with a house of lighter skeletal design, which still stands although it is no longer functional.

The headquarters of the Louisiana Jockey Club of New Orleans is seen in this photograph from the late nineteenth century. Designed by James Gallier, Jr., and built in 1865 for the prominent Luling family near Bayou St. John, it was sold to the Jockey Club in 1871 when the club took over management of the Fair Grounds Race Course nearby. It served as the club's headquarters for the next 20 years and still stands today, but is not open to the public.

Three women harvest sugarcane by hand in southern Louisiana in this photograph from the 1880s. Sugarcane has been a leading agricultural product for southern Louisiana for nearly 300 years, since its introduction by the Spaniards in the 1700s. Etienne de Bore, the first mayor of New Orleans, revolutionized the industry by being the first to product granulated sugar. Today most sugarcane is harvested by machinery.

In this image from the late nineteenth century, horse-drawn wagons deliver produce and other goods to the French Market in New Orleans. Begun in 1791 during the Spanish colonial era and still doing business on the same site, the French Market is the oldest city market in the United States. Long before the advent of prepackaged foods, people bought their produce fresh from the farm at public markets like this one.

The exterior of the A. Albert & Son Photographers and Stationer store in Alexandria is seen in this image recorded in 1886. By today's standards, early photography was very crude, requiring heavy glass plates and other encumbrances, but in its time it was a revolutionary method of permanently capturing visual images. Before personal cameras were introduced into the marketplace, professional photographers were always very much in demand.

Horse-drawn streetcars roll up and down the streets on both sides of the old French Market in this image, sharing busy thoroughfares with horse-drawn carriages bringing produce to the market. This photograph was taken by legendary photographer William Henry Jackson (1843–1942), whose landscapes of the Rocky Mountain West were among the first images recorded from that part of the country. He is perhaps best known for his iconic 1873 photograph of Colorado's Mount of the Holy Cross.

A firemen's parade is seen in Thibodaux in this image from around 1886. During a time when most structures were built of wood and most methods of illumination were flame-generated, fire was a constant threat to lives and property. Fire fighters were a very important component of every community and they often used parades on special occasions to publicly display their latest mobile firefighting apparatus.

A horse-drawn wagon bearing the casket of former Confederate States of America president Jefferson Davis rolls along a downtown street in New Orleans in December 1889. Born in 1808, Davis served as Secretary of War under President Franklin Pierce and in the U.S. Senate before becoming the only president of the secessionist states. He died in New Orleans on December 6, 1889, and was initially buried in Metairie Cemetery, then was moved to Richmond, Virginia, in 1893.

Crowds jam the wide breadth of Canal Street in New Orleans to watch the Rex parade on Mardi Gras Day around the turn of the century. Mardi Gras, meaning "Fat Tuesday" in French, is always the day before Ash Wednesday, which begins the Lenten fasting season that precedes Easter, 45 days later. Rex, a parading organization founded in 1872, features the "King of Carnival" on a special thronelike float on Fat Tuesday.

The ruins of Napoleonville are seen after a disastrous fire. Named after the French emperor who sold Louisiana to the United States and designated the seat of rural Assumption Parish, Napoleonville was hit by two conflagrations—on November 1, 1884, and again on December 2, 1894.

The Louisiana Sugar Exchange Building, which stood on the corner of Bienville and Front streets adjacent the New Orleans riverfront, is seen here in 1890. The Exchange was established to set prices and quality standards for its namesake product and was a key center for the commercial sugar trade in the late nineteenth and early twentieth centuries. The building was demolished in 1963.

Traders gather on the floor of the Louisiana Sugar Exchange along with bags of sugar readied for market here in 1890. Sugar is still a leading crop and manufactured product of Louisiana, but the importance of the Exchange declined as government regulations stabilized market prices in the mid-1900s.

The first electric-powered streetcars in Shreveport make their grand appearance on October 4, 1890. Curious onlookers watch the parade of the new vehicles at the corner of Texas and Market streets in the city's downtown area.

With one of the most ornately decorated exteriors of any building in downtown New Orleans, the Cotton Exchange was a hub of activity centering on this key agricultural crop in the late nineteenth century. Like the Sugar Exchange, it was established in 1871 as a central clearinghouse to set uniform cotton pricing and quality standards. This building was replaced with another structure in the early 1920s that still stands, today housing a hotel.

An electric streetcar rolls up St. Charles Street in downtown New Orleans late in the century. Until the entire length of St. Charles Avenue, from Canal Street to the Mississippi River, was given its present uniform name, its downtown section was designated St. Charles Street. Vintage streetcars still traverse the St. Charles Avenue Line, following the same route originally laid out in 1835.

The Old State Capitol in Baton Rouge stands fortress-like in the mid-1890s. Designed by architect James Dakin and located on a bluff overlooking the Mississippi River, its Gothic Revival, European castle-like exterior prompted author Mark Twain to ridicule it as "pathetic." Abandoned in 1932 when the newer, larger Capitol opened nearby, it is now a National Historic Landmark and revered as an architectural masterpiece. It houses a museum devoted to Louisiana's political history.

The Old United States Mint on Barracks Street on the edge of the French Quarter, New Orleans. Founded in 1839, the mint was still operating when this photograph was taken. It has the distinction of being the only mint to product both United States coins and coins of the Confederate States of America. During its years of operation, the Mint produced more than 427 million gold and silver coins of nearly every denomination, with a total face value of over $307 million. The mint still stands today as a unit of the Louisiana State Museum, and portions of it are open to the public. Many of the types of coinage minted there can be seen inside the museum, along with original equipment used to manufacture the currency. The Old Mint also houses other artifacts, including an extensive jazz collection.

In 1897, workers at the Old U.S. Mint punch out metal blanks on which images will be stamped in the manufacture of coins to be circulated as official currency.

Delegates to Louisiana's 1898 State Constitutional Convention convene in the legislative chamber of the Old State Capitol in Baton Rouge. This Constitutional Convention enacted many of the Jim Crow laws enabled by the U.S. Supreme Court's "separate but equal" ruling in the 1896 *Plessey v. Ferguson* decision, based on a New Orleans test case. The last of the Jim Crow laws were replaced by the most recent constitutional convention, held in 1974.

A group of nuns, Sisters of the Holy Family, gather for mass late in the 1890s. One of the few Roman Catholic orders made up of African-American women, the Sisters of the Holy Family was founded in 1837 by Sister Henriette DeLille, who is now being considered for sainthood by the Catholic Church. Today with 200 members, the order operates schools for poor children, nursing homes, and retirement centers.

People mill around the front entrance of the Lafourche Parish Courthouse in Thibodaux in this image from the turn of the century. Settled in the 1700s by French Acadians exiled from Canada (nicknamed "Cajuns"), the mid-sized city was named for Henry Schuyler Thibodaux, who owned a nearby plantation and was acting governor of Louisiana in 1824. The courthouse, built in 1860 on land donated by Thibodaux, still stands today.

Booms of Calamities

(1900–1919)

The elaborate Corinthian columns inside the old U.S. Customs House are featured in this image from around 1900. Located on Canal Street in New Orleans a few blocks from the river, the Customs House was built between 1848 and 1881 and housed the local customs office and other federal offices. Designated a National Historic Landmark in 1974, it reopened in 2008 as the Audubon Insectarium, the largest freestanding American museum dedicated to insects.

The old City Hall on St. Charles Avenue in New Orleans is shown here as it looked around 1900. Also known as Gallier Hall after its architect, James Gallier, Sr., it was built in the 1840s in the Greek Revival style and served as New Orleans' City Hall until the mid-1950s. It still stands today and is used for formal city functions. Many of New Orleans' most famous people have laid in state here, prior to burial.

Seen here fronting on Jackson Square around 1900, the Cabildo dates to the mid-1790s and was the seat of the Spanish colonial government in New Orleans prior to the Louisiana Purchase, which was signed in one of the Cabilo's rooms in 1803. Serving today as a unit of the Louisiana State Museum, the Cabildo was the scene of a fire in 1988 that destroyed its upper floors and cupola. They were rebuilt to the exact standards of the old building.

President William McKinley makes one of his final speeches from the balcony of the Cabildo during a visit to New Orleans in May 1901. An audience is seated in Jackson Square in front of the building to hear the speech. McKinley told the crowd, "My visit has been delightful," and he vowed to return soon, but on September 6 he was shot by a crazed anarchist while attending the Pan-American Exposition in Buffalo, New York, and died eight days later.

A group of young boys pose on and around a mule-drawn cart near the French Market in this early-nineteenth-century image. Empty wooden produce crates and produce displays, including bananas and other fruit, are visible in the background.

Streetcars roll side by side along St. Charles Street in downtown New Orleans in this view from around 1901. The streetcars seen in the picture were replaced in the early 1920s by the Perley Thomas Series 900 models, which still roll along the length of St. Charles Avenue today. The car at right is headed for Dryades Street, which at the time was the hub of retail commerce for the city's African-American population. Only one set of tracks remains today on this section of St. Charles for streetcars heading uptown.

The old New Orleans Public Library on St. Charles Avenue at Lee Circle. Built with a gift of $250,000 from wealthy industrialist-philanthropist Andrew Carnegie in 1908, the library was a distinctive architectural landmark whose loss was lamented when it was razed in the 1960s and replaced with a modern glass-and-steel structure that would, for a time, house the K&B drugstore chain headquarters.

Members of what appears to be a family pose in front of a fruit stand in New Orleans, possibly the French Market, sometime in the new century. Produce vending was very often a family-run business in New Orleans, particularly among the recent immigrants to the city.

President Theodore Roosevelt was on hand to address the Second Annual Banquet of the New Orleans Board of Trade during his visit in 1904. Roosevelt, who had succeeded the assassinated President McKinley three years earlier, was the second Chief Executive to visit New Orleans while in office. The city has been visited by every sitting president since.

Streetcars line up three abreast on the "neutral ground" of Canal Street in 1907. The busy hub of downtown New Orleans, Canal Street, for many years, featured upscale department store chains and was a fashionable shopping mecca, as well as an entertainment district lined with movie theaters. Many of the former department stores have since been converted into major chain hotels and condominiums, and plans are in the works to restore the old theaters.

The Rex parade moves along a very crowded Canal Street on Mardi Gras Day 1906. Every year a prominent member of the city's business community would be chosen to "reign" as Rex for the day, nicknamed "the Lord of Misrule." By tradition, the King of Carnival is toasted by the mayor outside Gallier Hall on St. Charles Avenue, which, for 100 years, served as the New Orleans City Hall.

The famous magician and escape artist Harry Houdini sits on a cotton bale on the New Orleans riverfront in 1907 talking to a man who is having his shoes shined. A riverboat is visible in the background. Houdini, whose real name was Erich Weiss, was born in Hungary in 1874. He traveled widely throughout the United States promoting his death-defying stunts, including escaping while being submerged upside-down in water and chained.

The campus of Louisiana State University in Baton Rouge as it appeared in 1909. The flagship college of the Louisiana State University System, the LSU campus in Baton Rouge was founded in 1860. Its first superintendent was General William T. Sherman, later a Civil War hero for the Union. Today's LSU campus occupies about 650 acres and encompasses 250 buildings. LSU Tigers football, which began in 1893, won national championships in the 1958, 2003, and 2007 seasons.

This rooftop panorama of downtown New Orleans offers a look at the city as it appeared in 1909.

A woman separates an egg in a kitchen in Crowley around 1910. The image was part of a series titled "Modern Cooking" by J. G. Ewing, a noted photographer of the day.

The packet steamboat *St. James* takes on passengers in New Orleans for a 350-mile round trip to False River, above Baton Rouge, around 1910. By the early 1900s, steamboats plying the Mississippi and other western rivers began to lose their importance as railroads and other methods of ground transportation prevailed. Sightseeing excursions became a way of replacing revenues lost on cargo and passenger transport.

This shot was taken of the old French Market in New Orleans around 1910 Before the advent of supermarkets later in the twentieth century, people bought their produce directly from outdoor markets, usually early in the morning while the goods were still fresh. The French Market was extensively renovated in 2008 and is still very popular today, especially with restaurant chefs.

A steam train on the Louisiana & Arkansas Railway rolls along the tracks near Minden in northern Louisiana. Incorporated in 1898, the L&A ran from Hope, Arkansas, to Shreveport and New Orleans with branches serving Vidalia, Louisiana, and Dallas, Texas. Originally a freight line, it began passenger service in 1928 and ended it 40 years later. The L&A was bought out by the Kansas City Southern Lines and the name was discontinued in the 1960s.

A nine-year-old boy named Johnnie shucks oysters under the watchful eye of the shucking boss, also known as a padrone. Workers, young and old and of all races and nationalities (many of whom were recent immigrants) worked in the shucking and canning shed of Dunbar, often from 3:00 a.m. to 5:00 p.m. with only half an hour off for lunch. Many of Dunbar's temporary residents migrated there from Baltimore, Maryland.

Oyster shuckers, most of them children, are seen working in one of the canning sheds in Dunbar. Trained as a sociologist, Lewis Hine used his camera to document the often deplorable conditions of American laborers and recent immigrants. The photos he took of child labor conditions in the early 1900s shocked the nation and helped enact laws establishing minimum age requirements for workers. The Dunbar settlement which, at its peak, housed about 300 workers, no longer exists.

Students are seated in a bookkeeping class at Louisiana Industrial Institute and College in Ruston in the early 1900s. Founded in 1894, it became Louisiana Polytechnic Institute in 1921, and finally Louisiana Tech University in 1970. Today it is best known for its engineering programs and its athletics, especially men's football and women's basketball. At last count, Louisiana Tech was attended by students from 46 states and 68 countries, with a total enrollment of nearly 11,000.

Students work in the campus machine stop at Louisiana Industrial Institute and College in Ruston, acquiring hands-on industrial training the early 1900s. Technical colleges like this one grew in importance and popularity in the late 1800s and early 1900s as the Industrial Age increasingly demanded these kinds of mechanical skills.

A large crowd of African-Americans gather in New Orleans in 1912 to hear famed educator and social reformer Booker T. Washington give a speech. Many spectators stand on railroad boxcars in the background. During the Jim Crow segregationist era of the early 1900s, Washington (1856–1915) was the voice of moderation in seeking to help African-Americans improve their social status and working skills. He helped found the Tuskegee Institute in Alabama for that purpose in the 1880s.

Cinderella, starring Mabel Taliaferro, showed at a main street theater in Shreveport around 1913. The most famous theater in Shreveport was the Municipal Memorial Auditorium, where the *Louisiana Hayride* show would be staged between 1948 and 1960. Simultaneously broadcast over 25 radio stations, the *Hayride* helped spotlight up-and-coming country-western and rock stars like Hank Williams, Elvis Presley, Johnny Cash, Webb Pierce, Jim Reeves, Governor Jimmie Davis ("You Are My Sunshine"), and many others.

Floodwaters from the swollen Mississippi River inundate the streets of Alsatia in East Carroll Parish in 1912. The building is probably a combination general store and post office, which was common in small towns at that time. The population of the eastern portion of this rural agricultural parish in the extreme northeast corner of Louisiana was displaced by the flood and had to be evacuated. This photograph and especially the two that follow capture the misery faced by residents of rural areas along the Mississippi who were vulnerable to flooding prior to construction of levees.

Children and their parents cook government-issued rations in a makeshift camp following the flooding that occurred in East Carrol Parish in April 1912. According to historical records, more than 1,000 square miles of active farmland went under water, in some cases as deep as six feet.

Evacuees from the April 1912 flood in East Carroll Parish board government-chartered steamboats along the Mississippi River. Most of the evacuees were transported about 40 miles downriver and temporarily housed in a cotton warehouse in Vicksburg, Mississippi, until the floodwaters subsided. This flood and two others that followed in 1913 and 1927 led to improved levee construction along most of the length of the lower Mississippi by the Army Corps of Engineers.

Governor Luther Hall (1869–1921) is seated at center in this 1913 group portrait of the governor and the Louisiana Supreme Court. Prior to serving as governor from 1912 to 1916, Hall was a state senator, a state district judge, and a state appellate judge. For the three years prior to his death he was the state's assistant attorney general. Other justices serving at that time and seen here include Frank A. Monroe, Oliver O. Provosty, Alfred D. Land, and Walter B. Sommerville.

A messenger boy delivers a telegram through the streets of New Orleans in November 1913. Lewis Hine was still traveling the country, pictorially documenting instances of child labor. He wrote, "The telegraph companies are trying to obey the law and few violations occur." This messenger boy appears to be old enough to handle the job and seems to confirm Hine's assessment.

The old Caddo Parish Court House in Shreveport as it appeared around 1916. Built in 1855, the red-brick building with its distinctive dome topped by a cupola briefly served as the Louisiana State Capitol after the fall of Baton Rouge during the Civil War. It remained in use until it was replaced with a white-marble structure resembling a wedding cake in 1928.

Soldiers relax at Camp Beauregard in 1918. The camp was located in Pineville, across the Red River from Alexandria, and was abandoned after the war in 1919 but returned to the government in 1940 for use as a World War II training area. Named for the New Orleans–born general whose battalion fired the first shots of the Civil War at Fort Sumter, the camp's hot, muggy weather made it a logical training location for American troops destined for service in similar climates. Today it is headquarters for the 225th Engineer Brigade, the largest engineer group in the army, and is also a National Guard training site.

A group of men stands beside a navigation lock near Mermenteau in Acadia Parish. Located on the Mermenteau River and Bayou de Cannes, Mermeneau is now the site of a shallow-draft port facility roughly midway between the larger municipalities of Jennings and Crowley. Hydraulic engineering was in the process of replacing manual labor in the operation of canal locks around the time this image was recorded.

Oil field workers pose at the foot of a drilling derrick in northern Louisiana around 1920. Drilling for oil became a big industry in the state's northwestern quadrant, centering on Shreveport, in the early 1900s. Wells in the north began to dry up by the 1920s but, not long afterward, oil was discovered in the Gulf of Mexico and the industry's focus shifted to the southern part of the state.

The Roaring Twenties and a Great Depression

(1920–1935)

Haynesville's main street is full of activity in this photograph from around 1920. Horse-drawn carriages and automobiles share the street during the heyday of the oil boom in northern Louisiana. Haynesville, in Clairborne Parish, just a few miles south of the Arkansas state line, was on the eastern edge of a vast subterranean oil reservoir that stretched into Texas. The boom was short-lived, as drilling drained much of the reserves within a ten-year span.

A group of five children play croquet on the lawn of the Playground of the Oaks Hotel in Hammond. Located about 50 miles northwest of New Orleans, Hammond was once a getaway destination for wealthy New Orleanians who had the means to leave the city during the hottest months of the year. Today is the crossroads of two interstate highways and the hub of a fertile strawberry-growing region.

Students pose in front of Minden High School in Minden in this early-twentieth-century group portrait. The school is still in use today, following extensive renovations completed in 2007. The seat of Webster Parish, 28 miles east of Shreveport, Minden was founded in 1836 and named for a city in Germany. Famed country-western singer Hank Williams was married there on October 18, 1952, three months before his death. Minden is also the home of Northwest Louisiana Technical College.

A streetcar rolls toward the busy intersection of Texas and Market streets in Shreveport's downtown business district in 1921.

Scene in the business district of Lafayette in 1921. Lafayette lies in the center of a region settled by French Canadians, who were forced into exile by the victorious British after they assumed control of Canada following the French and Indian War in the mid-to late 1700s. The term "Cajun" is a shortened form of *Acadian,* which describes the region of Canada bordering Nova Scotia and New Brunswick from which they were driven out.

Scene in downtown Monroe in 1921. The main city and population center of northeastern Louisiana, it was named for James Monroe, President Thomas Jefferson's special envoy who helped negotiate the Louisiana Purchase from France in 1803. He later became the fifth President, serving from 1817 to 1825. The city of Monroe lies on the Ouachita River, across from its "twin city," West Monroe, and is the seat of Ouachita Parish.

Enthusiastic Louisiana State University football fans pose inside an early convertible with a papier-mâché tiger mounted on the hood. "Mike the Tiger" has long been the mascot of the LSU Tigers, and these fans were in Shreveport for the 1921 gridiron match-up between LSU and the University of Arkansas Razorbacks. LSU won, 10–7. With a record of 33 wins, 19 losses, and 2 ties, the school currently holds the lead in this intercollegiate rivalry with the University of Arkansas which dates back to 1901.

A 1923 rooftop panorama of Lake Charles. The chief population center of southwestern Louisiana, Lake Charles recovered from a disastrous fire in 1910 that destroyed more than seven downtown city blocks. Today it is the fifth-largest city in the state and a center for gaming, drawing residents from nearby Texas to its floating casinos along the Calcasieu River.

High school and transfer buses sit parked outside the old, no-longer-standing high school in Plain Dealing in 1923. Situated in the northern part of Bossier Parish with a population of just over 1,000, Plain Dealing was named for a local plantation with the same name. The hottest recorded temperature in the state's history, 114 degrees Fahrenheit, was measure in Plain Dealing on August 10, 1936.

Students in their gym outfits are doing exercises or perhaps rehearsing a dance routine outside Patterson High School in Patterson in the early 1920s. Located in St. Mary Parish west of Morgan City with a population of more than 6,000, Patterson was settled in the early 1800s by Pennsylvanians of Dutch descent and originally known as Dutch Settlement. It was renamed for Captain John Patterson, a trader from Indiana who settled there in 1832.

This man is operating a mobile radio telephone from the backseat of a convertible in 1924, probably near the Mississippi River. Mobile telephone service was in its infancy in the 1920s and only a few individuals and official agencies had access to it.

Employees of Drexler's Ford dealership in Thibodaux pose in front of their building. Thanks to Henry Ford and his encouragement of assembly line production in his Detroit automobile plants, cars started becoming affordable to the average American by the 1920s. Fords were among the most popular cars of that time, a distinction they still enjoy today.

A paddle-wheel steamboat heads up a flotilla of seaplanes in the Mississippi River during the flood of May 1927. The aftermath of the flood led to a landmark federal decision to elevate and strengthen the levees along both banks of the lowest-lying sections of the Mississippi and to build two giant spillways to divert high water from the major population centers of Baton Rouge and New Orleans.

A troop of Boy Scouts distribute tobacco to African-American evacuees in a camp near Baton Rouge in May 1927. The Great Flood of 1927 had a strong sociological impact on American life. Many blacks who had lost their small farms to the flooding and were displaced migrated to northern cities in order to find work to support their families. Over the decades that followed, African-Americans gradually became the majority of the population in many northern cities.

This aerial shot of Alexandria in 1929 shows the domed City Hall in the center and the stately Hotel Bentley to the right. With a population of around 50,000, Alexandria (nicknamed "Alec" by the locals) is the commercial hub of the central Louisiana region. It was named for Alexander Fulton, a Pennsylvania businessman who received a land grant from Spain in 1785 and organized the settlement there, platting the town twenty years later.

Huddie Ledbetter is visible in the foreground of Prison Compound Number 1 at Angola State Penitentiary in July 1934. Better known as "Lead Belly," he became famous as a blues singer and guitarist after his musical talents were discovered during his years in prison. Born in Mooringsport in 1888, Lead Belly had a volatile temper and spent time behind bars more than once for murder and attempted murder. His most famous songs include "Goodnight Irene" and "Midnight Special."

The child of a strawberry picker stands in the doorway of the family's shack near Hammond in this image by Ben Shahn. A celebrated painter, illustrator, photographer, and teacher, Shahn (1898–1969) was also a social reformer with strong views on human rights. During the Great Depression, Shahn traveled the South, documenting rural poverty with his camera and brushes for the Farm Security Administration and the Resettlement Administration.

Hard Times, War, and Return to Prosperity

(1936–1949)

In this image by Ben Shahn, a group of young people gather on a New Orleans street around a man who has what appears to be a bear on a rope leash. During his photographic tour of the South, Shahn traveled with two other well-known photographers, Walker Evans and Dorothea Lange. A lifelong crusader for social justice, Shahn used his photographs as a way of attacking deplorable working conditions, bigotry, and other themes of the kind.

Following Ben Shahn in photographic documentation of the South was Walker Evans (1903–1975). Here, in December in the mid-1930s, Evans captures a moment in time at Canal and North Front streets—a time when coffee shops, oriental laundries, barbershops, upscale department stores, and smaller retail shops were the dominant businesses in downtown New Orleans. Today Canal Street consist mostly of hotels, souvenir shops, and discount clothing and footwear shops.

In this Walker Evans image, shops line Decatur Street in New Orleans in the vicinity of the French Market, the rooftops of which are seen at center in the background. Like Shahn, Evans is best known for documenting the conditions of rural poverty in the South, but he also photographed city life.

The La Branche House on Royal Street in the French Quarter was the subject of this image recorded in June 1938. Like many of the structures in the French Quarter, it dates from the first half of the nineteenth century. After New Orleans' capture by the Union during the Civil War, the house served as military headquarters for the occupation forces. Today it is one of the most photographed buildings in the French Quarter and is rumored to be haunted.

A Louisiana man attempts to put out a rice field fire near Crowley in Acadia Parish by beating it with a heavy cloth. This image and several that follow were shot by noted photographer Russell Lee (1903–1986) between September 1938 and January 1939. Best known for his work with the Farm Security Administration during the Great Depression, Lee shot many iconic images of day-to-day life in the Cajun country of southern Louisiana.

Two farmers take a break on sacks of rice outside a rice mill in Abbeville. The damp, swampy terrain of southern Louisiana around places like Abbeville, Crowley, and others made for ideal growing condition for the crop, and dozens of mills worked year-round to refine the product.

A truck delivers cases of Jax beer to a nightclub in Raceland as a group of young women watch from a doorway. Lying along scenic Bayou Lafourche in Lafourche Parish, about 40 miles west of New Orleans, Raceland is a community of about 5,000 people in the heart of the Cajun country.

A group of men are seen drinking beer in a bar in Pilottown. Bars, rural nightclubs, and dance halls were popular subjects of Russell Lee's body of work during his three-month stay in Louisiana. Pilottown is the southernmost settlement in the state, located near the mouth of the Mississippi River, and is only accessible by boat. It was named for the river pilots who often assembled there to escort foreign cargo ships up and down the river.

A group of young girls line dance across the wood floor of a roadhouse in Raceland as bemused male patrons look on.

Two guitarists perform in front of a group of Boy Scouts at the Rice Festival in Crowley in October 1938. The man seated is playing a Hawaiian-style guitar and the man standing is playing a dobro.

Young couples dance in the street at the Rice Festival as a crowd looks on.

A wide range of age groups enjoy a *fais-do-do* near Crowley in 1938. Cajun French that is loosely translated as "go to bed," the fais-do-do is a Cajun custom in which families get together at someone's house or barn to hear music, eat, dance, and socialize. The youngest children are put to bed while the older kids and adults get to enjoy the party. A Cajun band is playing at upper-right.

Cajun band members take a "beer break" between songs at the 1938 fais-do-do near Crowley. Traditional instruments in Cajun music include the accordion, fiddle, guitar, and a percussion instrument—often a washboard—but this particular band features two guitars and two fiddles. Cajun bands at that time usually sang in French, and most of them today do so as well, but with English translations. Today's zydeco music evolved from the Cajun music style.

A group of men raise a piano up to an elevated platform for a Cajun band contest at the 1938 Rice Festival in Crowley. A crowd gathers in the street in anticipation of the lively musical event.

A railroad crew takes a break on a siding in Port Barre. Settled in 1820 by the Barre, Nezat, and Roy families, the town was named for the Barre family patriarch, Alex Charles Barre. The town, in St. Landry Parish, was originally serviced by the New Iberia & Northern Railroad, which was later absorbed by the Missouri Pacific, and then by the Union Pacific.

Three older men sit around chatting on crude benches on the porch of a small grocery store near Jeanerette, Iberia Parish. A brand of cold medicine very popular during the era was known as 666, seen on the ad behind the men.

A brass band performs onstage during the 1938 Rice Festival in Crowley. Although Jim Crow laws at the time made enforced segregation of the races, all-black musical groups were allowed to perform in public places frequented by whites, and they were almost universally appreciated. Bands of mixed races, however, didn't come until many years later, after the Jim Crow laws were struck down by the court system.

Family members offer prayers at the graves of their deceased relatives in New Roads on All Saints' Day 1938. Visiting the final resting places of loved ones and making offerings of flowers and prayers on All Saints' Day (November 1), is an ancient Catholic custom dating back to the 600s and brought to Louisiana by the earliest French settlers. The custom is still observed throughout southern Louisiana today.

A group of men, women, and children gather around a booth at the South Louisiana State Fair to play Bingo. The South Louisiana State Fair was held in Donaldsonville, the parish seat of Ascension Parish, from 1913 to 1964. Today a scaled-down version of it is called the Sunshine Festival, after the nearby Sunshine Bridge over the Mississippi River. Concession stands in the background advertise caramel corn and plate lunches served on Holsum bread, which is still produced today.

Children ride on models of automobiles and fire engines on a merry-go-round at the 1938 South Louisiana State Fair in Donaldsonville as their parents look on in the background.

Children are transported home from school by a mule-drawn wagon near Transylvania in East Carroll Parish. In 1939, when this photograph was taken, motorized school buses had not fully replaced horsepower in this remote rural agricultural region. Taking advantage of its name, today the small town's general store sells vampire-related merchandise to tourists passing through on U.S. Highway 65, and the much-photographed Transylvania water tower has a vampire bat painted on it.

The McClung drugstore in Natchitoches is the subject of this June 1940 photograph by Marion Post Wolcott (1910–1990). As one of several photographers working under the auspices of the Farm Security Administration during the Great Depression, Wolcott pictorially documented day-to-day life and poverty in the rural South. FSA photographs influenced public opinion, boosting support for Roosevelt's New Deal policies and projects. Wolcott shot this image and the six that follow.

Locals in Natchitoches entertain themselves with guitar music. Natchitoches (pronounced nack-uh-tish) is the oldest permanent settlement in what was the Louisiana Purchase, founded on the Red River in 1714, four years before New Orleans. The Cane River plantations and many others sprang up in the area, which enjoyed an abundance of rich soil. The Red shifted course many years later, bypassing Natchitoches, but today the city's historic district is a mecca for tourism, thanks to the recently completed Interstate 49.

A wagon carrying young and older mulatto men and a lone woman returns from town with groceries and supplies near Melrose Plantation in Natchitoches Parish. One of half a dozen plantations along the Cane River, Melrose was the home for many years of noted folk painter Clementine Hunter (1886-1988). Hunter's primitive but colorful and expressive paintings of farm life in the region captured everyday scenes like the one shown in this Wolcott image.

Two crude wooden shacks and several smaller structures (including what appears to be an outhouse) sit alongside the railroad tracks in Roosevelt, in East Carroll Parish. So small it doesn't appear on most state maps, Roosevelt was probably named for Theodore Roosevelt, who hunted bears in the region during his presidency in the early 1900s. His cousin, Franklin D. Roosevelt, was president when this photograph was taken in 1940.

An elderly man with crutches rests on the front porch of a run-down shack near Natchitoches where he is selling live fish, including catfish.

Cars and pedestrians take to the busy streets of downtown Alexandria. The store at right advertises "Army Goods," which were undoubtedly popular items at the time, owing to the proximity of camps Beauregard and Claiborne. Camp Beauregard, which saw activity during World War 1, was reactivated the year this photograph was taken and used as a training base for soldiers who would be fighting in World War II a year later. Camp Claiborne was located about 10 miles south.

World War I hero Sergeant Alvin C. York of Tennessee (in the dark suit) addresses the 82nd Infantry Division at Camp Claiborne on May 7, 1942. Between 1939 and 1946 more than half a million soldiers trained at Camp Claiborne in Rapides Parish. Today the camp stands abandoned, and what remains is under the jurisdiction of the U.S. Forest Service.

A young dentist, aided by an assistant, examines a child's teeth in a New Orleans dentistry office in the early 1940s.

During Lieutenant General Walter Krueger's Third Army maneuvers in 1942, a group of civilian men supply the operations with gasoline directly from railroad tanker cars. The workers in the foreground fill up rows of five-gallon gasoline cans to be delivered to various field depots. The Third Army maneuvers began in summer 1941, before the U.S. entered World War II, and were held several times in subsequent years over a 3,400-square-mile area of western Louisiana.

Food rations for the solders of the Third Army training in western Louisiana are sorted in a grove of pine trees. Among the rations are frozen beef, ham, potatoes, and both fresh and canned vegetables. The open-backed, canvas-covered supply trucks are parked in the background. During the war nearly half a million men took part in army training exercises in western Louisiana.

This massive oil refinery in southern Louisiana in the mid-1940s was one of several in the state supplying fuel and lubricants to the Allied war effort. The refinery shown here featured three catalytic cracking units, better known as "cat crackers." The process breaks crude oil down into components that are refined into gasoline and other petroleum products. The American capacity to produce massive quantities of petroleum during the war is credited with helping hasten the Allied victory.

A law enforcement officer examines crime scene clues under a microscope in the Louisiana State Police Crime Lab in Baton Rouge around 1950.

Growing Pains at Midcentury

(1950–1969)

Around 1950, a group of children of varying ages sits on a bench reading books in the Bell City branch of the Calcasieu Parish Library.

Louisianians of Hungarian descent in colorful folk dresses and military-style uniforms dance the Csardas, a traditional Magyar dance, at the 1950 Hungarian Harvest Festival in Albany, Livingston Parish. Reported to be the largest rural Hungarian settlement in the United States, it was established in 1896 under the name Árpádhon (for Árpád, a ninth-century Magyar tribal leader, and "hon" for home[land]). The festival is still held today, following the end of the strawberry harvesting season.

Louisiana State Police officers of the "Stock Patrol" ride their horses down the middle of a Baton Rouge street in 1951. The Stock Patrol was started that year to remove livestock from highways, but their role expanded to assist as security during civil rights marches and live music concerts. State and local mounted police are still relied on today, especially during large-scale events like Mardi Gras, where their position high in the saddle gives them a better view of crowds.

This aerial photo taken in 1954 shows the newly completed Union Passenger Terminal in downtown New Orleans. The new station centralized passenger train operations, which had been scattered throughout the city. The UPT, which operates today as both an Amtrak and Greyhound Bus terminal, was built for a cost of $54 million and eliminated 144 track crossings from the city. The New Orleans skyline and the hairpin bend of the Mississippi River are visible in the background.

Water-skiers hang onto their towropes as they prepare to pass under a bridge during the 1955 Delcambre Shrimp Festival. Locally pronounced "Del-cum," this village of about 2,000 residents is 20 miles south of Lafayette and lies within both Vermilion and Iberia parishes. It is the hub of a large shrimping industry, and the Delcambre Shrimp Festival is held the third weekend in August each year to commemorate this heritage.

Here, in 1959, two visitors approach the obelisk of the Battle of New Orleans monument on the grounds of the Chalmette Battlefield Unit of Jean Lafitte National Historical Park in Chalmette. It was on this site that a ragtag army under General Andrew Jackson soundly defeated seasoned British troops in the final engagement of the War of 1812. The January 8, 1815 battle ended the last invasion on American soil by a hostile foreign army and helped propel Jackson into the presidency in 1828.

A festively decorated shrimp trawler bearing the name *Patricia* takes part in the annual Blessing of the Fleet at the Morgan City Shrimp Festival around 1960. A colorful ritual dating back several centuries to predominantly Catholic regions along the Mediterranean Sea, the tradition took root in the southern U.S. in the 1800s. A priest would come aboard a fishing vessel and bless it, offering a prayer for the safety of those aboard and for a bountiful harvest.

A group of bearded men take part in the 1960 Centennial celebration at the Morgan City Shrimp Festival. Incorporated in 1860 as Brashear City after early settle Walter Brashear, the name was changed to Morgan City to honor rail and steamship magnate Charles Morgan, who first dredged the Atchafalaya Bay Ship Channel to accommodate oceangoing vessels. Held annually on Labor Day weekend, today's Shrimp and Petroleum Festival honors Morgan City's two leading industries.

The King of the Yambilee Festival in Opelousas greets his Queen. Opelousas, the seat of St. Landry Parish, lies in the heart of a productive sweet potato region, and the Yambilee Fsetival is held the final weekend of October, around the time the yams are harvested. The festival was first held in 1946; the one shown here, some years later.

The historic steam locomotive *General* makes a stop in an unspecified rural location in 1962 during its Centennial tour through parts of the nation. The *General* figured prominently in the Civil War when a group of Northerners led by James Andrews commandeered the engine at Big Shanty, Georgie. Formerly the famous engine was preserved at Chattanooga, Tennessee, the northern terminus of its route from Atlanta. Today the engine and tender are on display at the Southern Museum of Civil War and Locomotive History at Kennesaw, Georgia.

Mardi Gras parade-goers wave their hands in the air, trying to catch "throws" from passing floats in 1962. The tradition of float riders throwing trinkets to the crowds along the parade route dates back to around the 1920s. Originally, glass beads were thrown but they were replaced with plastic beads in the 1960s. Today there are hundreds of different throws, ranging from aluminum coins (doubloons) and plastic cups to stuffed animals and much more.

St. Joseph Cathedral and its rectory in Baton Rouge as they appeared in 1964. Built in 1853 in the classic Gothic style and consecrated as a cathedral in 1970, St. Joseph's is the home church of the Bishop of the Baton Rouge Diocese.

The 1965 Magnolia Queen of the Yambilee Festival and members of her court ride through the streets of Opelousas in the "Grand Louisyam" parade. The award-winning float in the parade, it was sponsored by the Black Angus Restaurant and decorated by Yam Boosters. A uniformed soldier walks alongside the float and men on horseback ride behind it.

Spectators gather along a main street in Crowley to watch the 1965 Rice Festival parade.

Former Louisiana governor Sam Houston Jones (1897–1978) poses with a group of young people wearing costumes representative of ancient Americans as the 1966 dedication of a historical marker at the Old Camp Ground Cemetery near Sugartown, Beauregard Parish. Jones was from Beauregard Parish and his grandfather is buried in the Old Camp Ground Cemetery. Running as a reform candidate in 1940, Jones defeated the powerful Earl K. Long for the governorship but lost to him in 1948.

An antique car with campaign slogans saying "Vote Beanie" is parked alongside Cypress Lake on the campus of the University of Southwestern Louisiana in Lafayette. The occasion was probably an on-campus election in 1968. USL is now known as the University of Louisiana at Lafayette.

Tourists peruse a selection of paintings by a French Quarter artist in Pirate's Alley alongside St. Louis Cathedral in 1969. The narrow passageway's colorful name owes to New Orleans' history as a haven for pirates, most notably Jean and Pierre Lafitte, in the early 1800s. In 1925, writer William Faulkner lived in a small house on the one-block-long Pirate's Alley and wrote his first book there, *Soldier's Pay.* The house is preserved today as a bookstore and museum.

An aerial view of the Pentagon Barracks in Baton Rouge. The barracks, a military complex on the grounds of the State Capitol, stands on the site of a fort first built in 1779. The armies of Spain, France, Great Britain, the U.S., and the Confederacy have all had a presence there at one point in time. In 1976 the barracks were placed on the National Historic Register.

A mule-drawn surrey takes riders through the streets of Breaux Bridge during the 1968 Crawfish Festival. Proclaiming itself the "Crawfish Capital of the World," Breaux Bridge, in St. Martin Parish, draws many more people than its population of 8,000 during the popular festival celebrating the state's "Official Crustacean." The festival is held annually during the height of the crawfish season in late April and early May.

Among the most popular activities at the Breaux Bridge Crawfish Festival are the crawfish races. Bettors gather around the table during the 1969 festival, putting money down on the crustacean they think is going to win, while spectators gather on the outer ring to cheer them on.

Students gather around the Quadrangle at Louisiana State University in Baton Rouge in 1969. Like most colleges and universities around the United States during this time, LSU experienced its share of on-campus radical political activity. Sports—especially football—still reigned supreme. The Tigers played in eight major bowl games between 1961 and 1970, winning six of them.

The "Singing Christmas Tree" lights up the night sky in Natchitoches in December 1969.

Notes on the Photographs

These notes, listed by page number, attempt to include all aspects known of the photographs. Each of the photographs is identified by the page number, a title or description, photographer and collection, archive, and call or box number when applicable. Although every attempt was made to collect all data, in some cases complete data may have been unavailable due to the age and condition of some of the photographs and records.

Printed in the USA
CPSIA information can be obtained
at www.ICGtesting.com
JSHW072021140824
68134JS00042B/3736